AF808975

INTELLECTUAL PROPERTY MANAGEMENT

FOR TECHNOLOGY PROFESSIONALS:

A PRIMER

Donald W. Wyatt

ISBN: 978-0-692-530214

CONTENTS

Chapter 1: Why Did I Write This Book?

When I was working on my MBA, I had the opportunity to attend a lecture from a local entrepreneur. He had earned his bachelor's degree in business and had started a pharmaceutical company. His startup company had many ups and downs, but in the end he was highly successful.

Like most startup companies, startup pharmaceutical companies are cash poor until they reach a turning point (if they reach it) after which they generate lots of money. During this lecture, the entrepreneur explained in detail all the challenges his company had experienced and all the triumphs it had achieved. But through it all, he emphasized, the core driver of the decision making was the intellectual property.

After his talk, a classmate stopped me and asked, "You know intellectual property, don't you?" I replied that I do. I had earned a master's degree in intellectual property and had been working in technology companies as a patent attorney and in management for almost 20 years.

My classmate then asked, "When do we learn about this in our MBA program?" I replied that we don't.

We then began to discuss why business schools generally do not teach intellectual property management, even though many of their students will go on to technology companies for which intellectual property will be an essential component of those businesses.

At best, I explained, business schools may invite an attorney (who may or may not have experience in intellectual property) to teach a catchall category called "business law." It is better to refer this category as "laws that are related to business," as these classes tend to be a disparate set of complex concepts giving a general understanding of many different laws. Rarely will a student receive a real understanding of intellectual property as it relates to business management.

I further explained that business professors generally do not understand intellectual property management and that most companies rely on attorneys to manage their intellectual property. Yet, attorneys are really technicians when it comes to intellectual property. Nearly universally, attorneys don't have the management experience or the business education to understand how to manage intellectual property at a strategic level. They are primarily on the operational side of intellectual property.

For example, I am aware of a chief patent counsel for a global pharmaceutical company who had been hired directly from a law firm. His perspective, informed by his experience at the law firm, told him that the primary purpose of patent attorneys was to draft and file patent applications. Therefore, to instill discipline and to define his group's success, he based review and reward for the patent attorneys nearly entirely on the number of patent applications created.

Individual attorneys working in that company told me that there appeared to be no direct connection to strategic business goals being addressed by each patent application. It was considered among some (if not most) patent attorneys that a numbers-driven reward system was not only a large waste of their talent but also an incredible waste of a company's money.

It is clear that the lack of sophistication of even senior executives greatly diminishes a company's ability to establish an informed process that clearly directs decisions toward achieving intellectual property goals. Informed senior executives should find that a tally of the number of patent applications drafted in a period of time has dubious value to the company. It is very telling that executives senior to this chief patent counsel were also seemingly unable to offer that perspective.

When I looked to find books on intellectual property management, I primarily found books written by lawyers explaining patents, trademarks, copyrights and trade secrets with a description of the mechanisms by which these are obtained. It is not surprising, therefore, that a business manager would come away from reading such a book quite mystified. Starting by studying the different legal categories of intellectual property would be tantamount to studying everything there is to know about bricks and yet still learn nothing about architecture (strategic) or even brick-laying (operational).

Thus a technology company may be left with a management team that does not have a core understanding of intellectual property management and a legal team that does not understand corporate strategy and business management. The gap in the knowledge of each creates a void of communication that leads to hugely unnecessary expenditures and sometimes inadequate intellectual property positions. More sophisticated concepts, like when and how to initiate an intellectual property lawsuit against a competitor, are less informed than they ought to be and sometimes launched without a complete strategic perspective on the assets at hand.

So how do technology companies manage their intellectual property? For startup companies, their efforts are primarily ad hoc. That is, management works closely with a law firm, which guides them on the fundamentals of what intellectual property they could obtain and how to manage their approach to specific situations with rivals. However, intellectual property on a day-to-day basis tends to run in the background and only reaches the senior management or board level as a general update or when a crisis develops. This approach is more of a pull system rather than a push system from a management perspective. Most information and perspective flows from the bottom to the top with little guidance or insight flowing down.

Among more established companies, the approach to intellectual property management can also be ad hoc but in a different way. A culture may develop within the company for managing intellectual property issues. There are committees and specific policies. However, most companies establish these procedures based upon exigencies of the moment. These measures are not adjusted as situations change. The policies become so infused with artifacts that they become anachronistic. The measures lose their meaning and value over time.

With employee turnover, their effectiveness diminishes as institutional memory of the origins of the policies are lost. The committees and decision making systems are generally not regularly updated, and certainly not updated based upon a deliberate evaluation of the strategic intellectual property goals and operational outcomes. To many business managers and executives, intellectual property is something managed by the lawyers and is a very large line item in their expenses. That is the totality of their understanding on the subject.

It is ironic that companies develop complex systems to strategically manage human resources, inventory, supply chain, customer channels and so on, and yet have next to no such sophistication for managing intellectual property.

So what does it take to turn this situation around? A few available books advise companies to treat their intellectual property as strategic assets. This is excellent advice. However, what is needed first is a core understanding of the nature of these assets and what specific steps to take to begin managing them effectively. Managing intellectual property as strategic assets is the long term goal, but beginning to understand how to manage intellectual property at all is the immediate urgency.

This book is intended as a first step in that direction. It is a primer that first explains what intellectual property is, why it exists and how is it used. After providing this background, this book explores the currently recognized legal categories of intellectual property. Finally, all of this knowledge is captured in a single, simple exercise. The goal is to prepare an intellectual property plan to capture the goals and operational status of the company's intellectual property. This plan includes a "dashboard view" of a company's intellectual property.

A dashboard view is a single page using charts, graphs and short text that summarizes the goals and status of your intellectual property strategy at a moment in time. The dashboard view starts from a chart, preferably entered into a spreadsheet or a database. This dashboard view gives a quick perspective on what intellectual property goals the company should pursue, and whether or not it is effectively pursuing that goal. The dashboard can also give perspective on where the company may be wasting resources on useless intellectual property efforts.

This book is truly a primer. It is designed to be read by all technology professionals, including scientists, engineers, lawyers, managers, investors and anyone studying these subjects. The goal is to provide core concepts with a heuristic method of analysis that can be modified according to the needs or creativity of the reader.

As this book is directed to readers from varying backgrounds, each reader will find parts of this book to be easily understood (or even mundane) and other parts more challenging. There are many additional subjects that are not addressed here. That information is for a future book, perhaps.

Intellectual property is a rich field full of opportunities for creative thinking and application. I hope you have as much fun reading this as I did writing it.

Enjoy!

Chapter 2: What Is Intellectual Property?

There are many definitions of intellectual property ranging from the highly technical to the user-friendly. Intellectual property is a relatively difficult concept to grasp because there is no physical reference. The concept is a notion of owning something that is intangible: you can't see it, you can't feel it, you can't smell it, but it may be essential to your company.

Probably the best beginner's definition is that intellectual property is "owning ideas." Intellectual property experts will cringe at this definition because the analogy breaks down under scrutiny. However, this definition will work for now.

But even if you contemplate the concept of owning an idea, you are left wondering, "What does that really mean?"

The best way to understand what it means to own an idea is to start by exploring what it means to own a thing. All of us walk around every day with the things we own. We own our shirts, we own our pencils, we own our shoes, and we even own our cars when we finally pay off the bank. However, if you were to ask a hundred people in the street, it is unlikely that you would find one person who actually understands what it is that gives them that ownership right.

A good way to understand the concept of owning something is to go through a lecture I have given to business students while I was living in China. As the lecture opens, I introduce myself and I pick a student at random. I ask the student if she has a cell phone and, of course, the answer is yes. I then ask if I can borrow the cell phone. Without exception she hands me her cell phone.

I then walk over to a second student, and I ask, "May I use this phone to call the President of the United States in the White House in Washington, DC?" More often than not, the second student will refer me to the first student who handed me the cell phone.

I then ask the second student, "Why do I have to ask the student who handed me the cell phone? After all, I'm the one holding the phone now; isn't possession the sign of ownership?"

The second student, of course, answers that I have no ownership rights and that I must speak to the owner. I then ask the class, "What makes her, the student who handed me the phone, the owner of this cell phone?"

Hands go in the air, and the first answer nearly invariably is that since she is the one who paid for the cell phone, she owns it.

I then engage in a little make-believe and tell them that I know she did not pay for the cell phone. In fact, her mother has given her the cell phone. So, if she did not pay for it, does she still own it? Confusion entails, but the students concede that payment does not establish ownership.

I then ask, "If possession and payment are not the definition of ownership, then what makes her the owner of this cell phone?" This question generally brings a pause. The next obvious answer is that she is the one with the right to use the cell phone. I then challenge this notion by switching subjects.

I ask the students if any of them own a car. Those who do own a car raise their hands. I then propose to them that the Shanghai government has decided that pollution is much too intense and that they are not allowed to start their cars.

I ask them, "If you can't use your car because you cannot start it, do you still own it?" Of course the answer is yes. Ownership and the right to use are two different concepts it appears. The confusion multiplies.

So if possession and payment do not clearly establish ownership, and the right to use is not the definition of ownership, what then is ownership?

Once, a student raised her hand and gave the right answer, "Ownership is the right to exclude others from using."

This answer is correct. The extent of your ownership of a thing is the extent of your ability to exclude others from using it. It is that simple.

Now that you better understand what it means to own thing, you can apply this to the concept of owning an idea. You own an idea when you can create a new one and exclude others from using it.

So what does owning an idea look like? Now I can introduce a concrete example, and the very first known patent is a good one.

The story comes from Florence, Italy, in the year 1421. At that time, the city was in a building boom. During this boom, the Florentines were importing a great deal of the marble that you can see on the beautiful white buildings of the city today.

Bringing the marble up the river on barges was the most efficient way to import this key material. Nevertheless, the system was slow, and it became a bottleneck for the plans of the city's managers. It was also expensive due to labor costs and the limited supply owing to slow delivery.

One of the barge owners, Filippo Brunelleschi, had an idea for a method to greatly improve delivery of the marble. His idea was to use a newly designed hoist built into his barge for lifting the marble onto the shore.

But this idea lead to a conundrum. If Brunelleschi began using the hoist, his competitors would see what he was doing and copy it. The resulting increase in the volume of marble delivered would cause a price reduction. Not only would he lose the financial benefit of using his hoist, but he would also be forced to deliver more marble at lower prices in order to keep his revenue stable.

What he needed was the ability to benefit from increasing the volume of his marble delivery while selling it at the current prices. He needed to be the only one using his hoist idea. He needed exclusive use of his invention. That is, he needed to own his idea by excluding others from using it.

Without revealing his plan, Brunelleschi approached the town managers and explained his dilemma. Importantly, he also explained the benefit his secret invention would have for the city in the increased delivery rate of marble.

The city managers wisely recognized that although they would get a small increase in the delivery of marble from one vendor, it would not be enough of an increase to affect the pricing or overall volume of marble being delivered. The city would not benefit much from granting Brunelleschi sole rights to use his invention.

This analysis revealed their own conundrum. They surely wanted the increase in volume resulting from speedy delivery. The invention could provide that benefit. However, Brunelleschi refused to disclose or use his invention if he could not benefit financially. Yet, the city could not benefit much unless all the delivery companies were using Brunelleschi's invention. Exclusivity to Brunelleschi would prevent them from benefiting from the idea.

They solved the problem with a time limit. The bargain they struck was to provide exclusivity to Brunelleschi for three years. After those three years, the invention would become public, and the city's benefit from the invention would begin after the exclusivity expired.

In this example, you can see how a balance can be struck between inventors with new ideas and the public who wish to benefit from those ideas. Inventors are encouraged to share their ideas by allowing them to exclude others from using those ideas (they "own their ideas") for a limited time. After this time period, the public benefits from wider application of the idea.

Unlike the ownership of things, the ownership of ideas is more often than not limited in time. Inventors are permitted to have exclusive use of their ideas for a period of time. After this exclusivity period, anyone in the public can use and benefit from the idea.

The creator of the idea is being paid for having disclosed the idea through an exclusive use of the idea. This situation lasts for a period of time. After this time period is over, payment by society to the inventor is completed and the idea is thereafter dedicated to the public.

With this theoretical explanation and the concrete example, you should now have a better understanding of what it means to own an idea. More importantly, you should be forming a better understanding of the nature of intellectual property.

Now would be a good time to think about some of the intellectual property with which you are familiar. Do you work for a company that speaks about its intellectual property? What ideas are captured within it? Are there time limits involved?

For some it is too soon in this book for such contemplation. After reading a few more chapters in this book the concepts may become clearer. For others the answers to these questions may offer new insight into their company's assets.

However, the question now arises, in the larger scheme of things, why does intellectual property exist?

Chapter 3: Why Does Intellectual Property Exist?

Now that you have a working understanding of intellectual property, you can dig a little deeper to explore the reason that intellectual property exists as a concept. In short, it is because ideas have value.

A good way to approach an understanding of this concept is to return to an analysis of the ownership of things. Why do we have the concept you can own a pencil? Why do we own clothing?

The simplest explanation will work for our purposes here. By granting ownership (that is, the right to exclude others) we impart value to these items. When we can exclude others and when they want the item, they will value that item. When an item has value, it could become the basis of trade.

For example, if you think back to the example in which I borrowed the cell phone from a student, you can imagine the feelings of everyone in the room when I asserted ownership and questioned her ownership. All of the students can be expected to have experienced a small feeling of loss, especially when they were unable to clearly articulate why I was not the owner.

The idea that the student might not have the right to exclude others from her cell phone was disconcerting to them.

If we together had not found the true meaning of ownership, we very well may have concluded that she had no rights at all. If the owner of the cell phone has no rights, then the cell phone has no value.

To make a clearer point, I return to the lecture to the students. At the point at which the class comes to understand that ownership means the right to exclude others, I then asked the class why we have such rights at all, and what would happen if I put a cell phone in my pocket and walked out the door.

The response was often cacophonous. Clearly every student was ready to call the police. But then I posed a further question.

Imagining the scenario unfolding, I asked them to consider what would happen next. Perhaps two detectives would arrive a few hours later. Each student would be questioned as to what they had seen. The two detectives would then begin a search for me and the missing cell phone. After a successful search, the police would take me to the station in handcuffs and imprison me. The student's cell phone would be returned.

I then ask the students to imagine the expense of that process, and to compare that expense to the cost of just giving the student a new cell phone. Wouldn't it be much easier and cheaper to let me keep her cell phone and for society to give her another?

Clearly, in the immediate circumstance the answer to the question is "yes."

However, if our solution to theft is free replacement of the missing items, then the value of the items we own tracks to zero. If replacement is the cure for theft, there is no value in excluding others from our items. We cease to "own" them as the value of excluding others disappears.

Once excluding others from our items tracks to zero, so does the value of those items. There can be no exchange, there can be no trade and, therefore, there can be no economy. Why would someone trade (exchange money) for an item that when it is taken, it just gets replaced? Why pay for something you can take for free?

As that scenario plays out, you realize that cell phones would simply never have existed at all. Nobody would bother to produce something that will have no value.

So ownership, the right to exclude others from using items, is fundamental to the notion of having an economy. Without trade and economy, no cell phones would even exist.

I am at risk of being overly simplistic here, but the purpose of this discussion is to transition to the concept of intellectual property. As I re-pose the question "Why does intellectual property exist?" our answer is the same as why the ownership of items exists.

The notion of intellectual property exists because it advances the economy by imparting value to ideas. Intellectual property creates a trade of ideas similar to the trade of items and things, which ultimately has an economic benefit to society.

When we allow people to own items and things, we create value in things which greatly enhances the number of useful things produced. Likewise, when we allow companies and people to own their ideas, society greatly enhances the number of useful ideas that become available.

To further illustrate this concept, you can return to the challenge for Brunelleschi and the city of Florence. You understand that Brunelleschi's idea would enhance the economy of Florence. But you also understand that the he has no incentive to give away his idea to the public with no benefit to himself.

As you recall, the solution entailed a temporary right to exclude others before the benefit transitions from the individual to the public. By giving Brunelleschi the right to exclude others, the city of Florence imparted value to his idea. By imparting value to ideas, the Florentines created a market for ideas.

There are fundamental characteristics of this deal that still carry through to our modern understanding of intellectual property. The first is an individual right to exclude. The second is the temporal nature of that right. Intellectual property rights should nearly always be understood as being temporary.

It is interesting to note that these two fundamental features of intellectual property were well known at the foundation of the United States as a country. The United States Constitution specifically grants Congress the power to give exclusivity to intellectual property for limited periods of time.

In fact, the Constitution requires Congress to grant such rights. However, by specifying that any rights granted must be temporary, the Constitution forbids Congress from granting intellectual property rights in perpetuity.

Thus, this document artfully captures these two fundamental notions of intellectual property in one simple clause: exclusivity and limited in time.

So a society will grant intellectual property rights for limited periods of time. Which rights are granted and for how long is a balance of the societal benefits/needs with individual benefits/needs.

Now you only need to better understand what kinds of ideas should be owned and under what circumstances. But first I will present how intellectual property can be used to advance the economy. That is, how is intellectual property used?

Chapter 4: How Is Intellectual Property Used?

While most people see intellectual property solely as a legal concept, it should more properly be viewed as set of business tools. You are not yet ready for me to address all the categories of intellectual property that are formally recognized today (the legal concepts). I will first present a broad overview of how intellectual property is used in modern technology companies (the business tools).

Professionals are limited only by their imagination as to how they can leverage the tools of intellectual property. However, technology companies primarily use three fundamental models. These are (1) pricing power, (2) defensive bargaining, and (3) direct revenue generation.

Please understand these categories to be a generalization permitting you to easily and accurately identify the value and purpose of any individual piece of intellectual property. Companies don't use only one intellectual property model to advance their business interests, and they can implement modified versions of any of them. Companies can and should use as many as possible of the three core models, and any other derivative model they can invent.

The First Model: Pricing Power

Pricing power is the use of intellectual property to generate market exclusivity zones around a product or service, allowing a company to use that exclusivity to increase revenues.

Though this model is called pricing power, note that it is the increase of revenue that is the issue here, not merely increasing prices. Revenues are higher with the intellectual property exclusivity than they would be without that exclusivity.

The market exclusivity zone created around the product or service may allow increased revenue through (1) increased prices without a loss of sales volume, but also could allow for (2) increased revenue through greater volume without the need to lower prices.

How Does It Work?

If a product or service has value to the consumer, obviously gaining a market exclusivity against competitors allows a reasonable increase in prices without a meaningful drop in sales volume, thus increasing revenue.

It is a little less clear how an exclusivity zone can be used to increase volume without reducing prices. Our prior example of Brunelleschi's invention in the city of Florence of a barge with a hoist is a good example.

Brunelleschi was granted a three-year period of exclusivity by the city of Florence for his invention. No other barge owners were permitted to install hoists into their barges during that period. The invention allowed an increase in efficiency of delivery of the product, but not an improvement in the product itself. Thus, the invention did not enhance the product itself in a way that would support an increase in price.

However, during those three years, the invention allowed our innovator to increase his own volume. Brunelleschi's exclusivity of the invention ensured that the overall volume in the larger market was changed very little. Therefore, we would not expect that the market price for the product would have a downward pressure while only a single player was using this invention.

The efficiency of delivery benefits this merchant while keeping the overall market value of the product stable. The inventor brings larger volumes to market with stable prices. Competitors are unable to match the volume without copying the invention. Prices remain stable, and the inventor's revenues go up.

Another example gives insight into the ability to raise prices without losing volume. Consider the old tried-and-true corkscrew. It works very efficiently, but requires using two hands and some strength to open a wine bottle.

Along comes an inventor with a single-hand cork puller. This tool is far easier to use. The value to the buyer depends on the value proposition (what value the consumer sees in using this product over other solutions). If it is very easy to use, consumers are likely to see a larger value proposition. They will pay far more for the single-hand puller than for the corkscrew. I will call that difference in value "the price gap."

However, the number of buyers placing a large value on the single-hand puller over the corkscrew is limited. Some people will be willing to pay, but others will not. Therefore, the inventor of the single-hand puller is interested in maintaining exclusivity over his invention. With only a fraction of the market willing to pay a premium price, the inventor will want to keep that fraction of the market to himself.

Exclusivity allows the inventor to pursue all the buyers willing to pay the price gap without competition. Lacking this exclusivity, multiple sellers will compete with each other on price, and the selling price of the single-hand puller will sell at a much smaller price gap. The value of the idea will diminish greatly.

So it is safe to say that:

-Intellectual property protection for inventions that increase the efficiency of production and/or delivery will generally permit the inventor to increase volume without having to reduce prices, and

-Intellectual property protection for inventions that increase the value proposition to the consumer by affecting the nature of the product generally permit the inventor to increase prices without concern over loss of sales volume.

Who Uses the Pricing Power Model?

Any company or industry can use the pricing power model. However, companies using pricing power as a dominant or exclusive model are commonly heavily regulated by the government and/or require intensive capital investment before a product can reach the market.

The pharmaceutical industry is a good example of this. These companies have a significant risk of failure after a long and expensive investment in research. These risk factors and barriers to entry require the expectation of good market conditions upon success. Without exclusivity provided by intellectual property, there is far less certainty of a successful outcome.

One of the main characteristics of an industry that uses the pricing power model is its great sensitivity to the expiration of the rights. Like a gold mine, the intellectual property in a pricing power model is a wasting asset. Just as the gold in a gold mine diminishes as it is being dug out, the ticking clock of intellectual property expiration gives finality to the value of the exclusivity.

In the pharmaceutical industry, when a new drug launches, it is a valuable product. However, the product experiences a severe drop in value when it has aged to the point that its exclusivity rights have expired. Revenue can drop from billions of dollars to thousands of dollars in just a few weeks to months, because this industry's products are so easily copied. Many industry players are ready to capitalize on the relatively easy, low-risk business of copying older drugs.

Companies using the pricing power model may also be sensitive to the expiration of intellectual property belonging to competitors.

When a piece of intellectual property provides exclusivity to a feature of a product, you can refer to that feature as being *covered by* the intellectual property.

Now, imagine a market having exclusivity divided among a few players. Each player has their own competing product and also has their own intellectual property covering their respective product. With only a few players, there is little pressure to compete on price.

Imagine also that there is little market value difference between the competing products (they all seem to work well enough). Therefore, when one of the players loses exclusivity rights through expiration, all of the products in that space will feel the effects of the entry of many cheap copies of the product. Heavier competition on price has been introduced into the market for these products. All players have lost pricing power.

For example, imagine a pharmaceutical company expending great effort and money to try to generate a product. The research and the management of government regulation are both expensive and sources of great risk of failure. At the end, the product is somewhat easy to copy. As the product is so easily copied, the primary and only protection this pharmaceutical company has to benefit from its efforts is intellectual property exclusivity.

Next, imagine that you are in a pharmaceutical company selling a highly effective allergy drug. It has value to the consumer because it does not make them as sleepy as the standard allergy drug. You call it non-sleepy allergy medicine.

You have exclusive rights to this particular drug. A handful of other companies are also selling similar non-sleepy allergy drugs. They have their own intellectual property exclusivity to their products. Consumers see a value difference between the drugs that do not make them sleepy and the standard allergy drugs (the price gap), but do not see much value difference among the non-sleepy allergy drugs.

There is little incentive for the few players to compete with each other on price during the time all these drugs have exclusivity to their owners. With only a handful of sellers, they compete through aggressive marketing. Each is attempting to grab the price gap at its maximum. They are not likely to compete in a way that would reduce this price gap.

However, as these drugs get older, at least one player will lose exclusivity through expiration. Many new players will enter the market with cheaper copies of that one aging drug.

Consumers will not see any value in the difference between the products that still have exclusivity and the one that no longer does. The price gap narrows for all products as the one product gets copied quickly and cheaply by many new players in the market. The market has changed for all players, not just the player whose exclusivity had expired.

Therefore, it is important to keep an eye on the expiration of intellectual property rights of your closest competitors when you are using a pricing power model. How will the expiration of their intellectual property rights affect your pricing power in the model? Do consumers see a value difference between your product and your competitors' products? Without a perceived value difference, the loss of exclusivity by your competitor will likely be your loss as well.

Another example of an industry that is highly sensitive to the expiration of intellectual property rights is the entertainment industry. Though not traditionally grouped with technology companies in the mind of the public, the entertainment industry is highly dependent upon new technology in the development of their products. Creative works like characters and storyline can be considered to be technology for our purposes.

Disney, for example, uses technology to develop new entertainment products with a high rate of success. Their ability to generate revenue, and, therefore, use a pricing power model of intellectual property, depends heavily upon one form of intellectual property called copyright.

In short, copyright exclusivity permits Disney to prevent others from freely distributing their creative products. Expiration of copyright could be devastating to the company.

In fact, when Disney's core copyrights on its original characters were coming due for expiration in 1998, the United States Congress extended exclusivity for all copyrights. Disney was so sensitive to the loss of a pricing power model that it was in the national interest to maintain those intellectual property rights.

How long the product will be in the market before it is replaced or directly copied is called the life cycle of the product. The expiration of the intellectual property often defines the end of a product's life cycle for pricing power model users.

Another way to analyze the same phenomenon is to assess when the price gap (as defined above) will significantly narrow. Is it because of new, improved products entering the market or is it due to the expiration of intellectual property rights? For pricing power industries, the life cycle of the product often corresponds to the term of exclusivity of the intellectual property.

Other industries have product life cycles that are defined by the entry of improved models with better features and functionality. As the new comes in, prices on the old drop precipitously and independently of intellectual property expiration.

How Do I Identify Intellectual Property as Suitable for the Pricing Power Model?

Without getting into the details of the current categories of intellectual property available (that is the next chapter), suffice it to say that intellectual property is generally directed to components of a product or service.

When the intellectual property describes something that permits the seller to produce more efficiently or deliver more (and/or faster), it is similar to the situation faced by Brunelleschi. In that case, the described feature was a delivery method. The applicability to a pricing power model is clear. The delivery methods permitted increased volumes without downward pressure on prices. This improvement produced increased revenue.

You must conduct a more complex analysis for pricing power model suitability when the covered feature is intrinsic to the product itself. The analysis turns on the ability to increase prices without losing sales volume when the covered feature modifies the product.

In these instances, an aspect of the product that is unique is usually identified as a covered feature. Describing this unique feature, the intellectual property can cover an aesthetic feature of the product or a functional feature. For example, it can be directed to the look, design features, or even a unique name. Alternatively, it can describe a unique way the product functions and/or a unique functional feature of the product.

Once this component is identified, it needs to be analyzed for whether or not the intellectual property directed to that component is suitable for a pricing power model.

In order to be suitable, the component covered by the intellectual property should:

1) Describe something unique to the function or aesthetic value of the product or service.

-The intellectual property will cover a key function of the product or service, or…

-On the other hand, the intellectual property may cover a unique name or other aesthetic feature. For example, it may be the shape of a bottle (think: ketchup bottles or window cleaner).

This criterion is easy to assess. It is a binary inquiry with a yes/no answer.

2) Due to the covered feature specifically, the product would be undesirable to substitute with alternatives.

This criterion is a little more complex to assess. It requires some understanding of the interests of the buyers.

For example, it is true for any product that easy substitution of an alternate product by the consumer lowers the value of that product. The strength of the application of intellectual property to a pricing power model is converse to the ease with which a buyer can substitute the component covered by the intellectual property.

For example, imagine that a company has exclusive rights to the use of powered switches to perform mathematical operations (e.g., a calculator or computer).

When intellectual property provides exclusivity, the suitability of this intellectual property to support a pricing power model is inversely proportional to the ease of substituting something lacking that technology (e.g., an abacus).

On the other hand, if the intellectual property covers something aesthetic (look or feel of the product, or a product's unique brand), its ability to be substituted by an alternate aesthetic is seemingly obvious. The marketing surrounding this aesthetic is critical.

If the purchaser connects the name of the manufacturer or even the look or feel of the product to the quality desired, they will connect this aesthetic to the value proposition of the product as a whole. Purchasers will have less incentive to seek alternatives.

As an example, people are attracted to the "Intel" name for computer processors. It is a name. It is an aesthetic feature that has no direct bearing on the function of the product. However, due to the marketing and quality control of the product, buyers expect that name to come with high quality. This expectation makes the unique identifier "Intel" suitable intellectual property for a pricing power model. People will pay more to get the quality implied by the Intel brand. Without that name/brand, buyers are less likely to pay as much.

Likewise, Apple has built its brand around the idea of quality and ease of use. Apple's repeated success in producing innovative products that are easy to use has created a significant price gap to most alternatives.

It can be argued that Apple was so successful in this approach that it achieved a new level of price gap. Apple was able to drive even higher levels of pricing through the use of limited releases of new products. Being a buyer purchasing a just-released product became a status symbol commanding large value propositions, even in the face of technical glitches of early-release products.

All of this value is captured in the brand name, "Apple". Without this intellectual property, the price gap could not have been created and the pricing power model would have failed.

Sunbeam provides a contrasting example. For many years this brand name carried the same reputation for kitchen appliances as Intel does for processors. However, senior management lost sight of the value of the investment in the brand and made significant changes to the product supply chain. They outsourced manufacturing to very low quality vendors, and the reputation of the products suffered accordingly. Sunbeam lost its premium market and has never recovered. Sunbeam no longer enjoys the same pricing power model to drive its revenues.

The pricing power model requires investment in the reputation of the brand when the intellectual property covers an aesthetic feature. The covered aesthetic feature represents that reputation.

As you capture a unique identifier for the product in a piece of intellectual property, you use branding to instill value in the identifier. By nurturing the right reputation, you can enjoy a pricing power model of revenue generation.

Keep in mind that consumers consider not only the quality of the product as it relates to their needs but also other factors, such as being cool, exciting, environmentally sound, and so on.

While it is difficult to imagine the average consumer being concerned about quality of functional features of a keychain, if that keychain says "Ferrari," it is more likely to sell at a higher price than other keychains. Thus, the pricing power model criteria are fulfilled.

There is an interesting exception to the criteria above in a particular circumstance. When (i) the coverage is of a key function of the product, (ii) the barrier to entry of competing products is high (think: a need for expensive government approval, strict government regulation of the use of the product, or a need for very rare skills to produce the product), (iii) the value of the product is very high, and (iv) the overall size of the market is quite small, then the second criterion above is possibly self-fulfilled. (Reminder: The second criterion is the need for substitutes for the covered function to be undesirable in the mind of consumers.)

For such a product, the high value of the product means the purchasers must believe that the quality and applicability of the product suit their specific needs. A substitute with alternate technology will have to prove itself before buyers will take the risk of substitution.

The barrier to entry for competitors means that new product sellers must both invest in producing the product and convince consumers that their alternate solution is just as good as the original. The overall small market means that even if a competitor succeeds in introducing its product, unless the product is clearly superior, the competitor will likely have to compete very heavily to make money.

In such a market, it is likely that only direct copies of the original product are worth the risk to introduce. Consumers will not yield to substitutes easily, and it is very risky to introduce a different product that may not capture the interest of the few buyers. Therefore, if the producer of the original product can get any intellectual property covering a component of the function of the product (whether that function is key or mundane), a pricing power model is likely to be achieved.

A likely example is in pharmaceuticals. Prescription drugs, before they are generic and easily copied, are nearly always valuable. Yet, the barrier to entry for another (non-copy) drug for the same disease is extremely high, often in the hundreds of millions of dollars. If the drug treats a relatively rare disease, then the overall market may be relatively small and not support the cost of developing a second, alternative drug for this disease.

In this case, copying the original drug is likely the only avenue for a competitor. Yet, if the original drug has any functionally related intellectual property, even if that functionality is easily substitutable (failure of the second criterion), no one is likely to invest in new product development to introduce even such a small change.

For example, a new method of dosing a drug is considered to be relatively weak subject matter for a pricing power model because it is so easy to design around. Yet, if that change means going through all the government approval process of a non-copy to serve a small market, then it is good enough coverage to support a pricing power model. The cost of introducing a near copy to the original is too high for the small reward of success.

But don't despair, even the mundane intellectual property will expire and copies can enter the market for everyone thereafter. It is better that treatments for rare diseases having small markets get an easier time achieving a pricing power model. That way, companies have an incentive to produce the first treatment for the disease and cheaper copies can follow later.

The Second Model: Defensive Bargaining

Defensive bargaining is a different way of exploiting intellectual property rights. Defensive bargaining is obtaining exclusivity rights that extend beyond your own products. It is the collecting of intellectual property rights that would be of interest to your competitors for the purpose of discouraging legal conflict over intellectual property rights against your own products.

The defensive bargaining intellectual property model and pricing power model are not mutually exclusive. It is quite possible, and even common, for those seeking to use a pricing power model to also collect intellectual property for a defensive bargaining model.

Who Uses the Defensive Bargaining Model?

Technology companies that exploit intellectual property primarily through a defensive bargaining model tend to be those in fast-paced industries. Industries experiencing quickly improving products constantly being introduced have difficulty generating intellectual property rights to a specific product that would be in the market long enough to use a pricing power model.

Viewed another way, the life cycle of their products tend to be defined more by the introduction of newer models with improved features and functionality rather than by the period of exclusivity provided by intellectual property. In these products, the traditional notion of pricing power comes primarily from the newness of the product and its desired features.

Technology companies working in such industries will want to have a library of such intellectual property rights.

How Does It Work?

The defensive bargaining model is a game of mutually assured destruction. When industry players own key intellectual property rights covering their competitors' products, they can insulate themselves from the legal hurdles caused by their competitors' intellectual property assets.

Imagine, for example, that one company has intellectual property to the way in which a mobile phone dials, while another company has intellectual property covering the way in which a mobile phone connects to a radio tower. Each company can use both of those features with impunity. After all, both will be left with mobile phones that do not work if they attempt to exclude one another from using their own particular feature.

As the imaginary example shows, even in fast-paced industries there can be many intellectual property rights directed to fundamental underlying inventions that carry over from generation to generation of products. However, companies need to have the freedom to pursue the latest generation of product unhindered by the intellectual property rights of their competitors.

How Do I Identify Intellectual Property as Suitable for the Defensive Bargaining Model?

The characteristics of intellectual property suitable for the defensive bargaining model are somewhat simpler than for the pricing power model. It is necessary for the coverage of the intellectual property to extend beyond your own product to those of your competitors. In fact, the intellectual property may not cover any feature of your own product. As long as it covers a feature of your competitors' product(s), it is suitable for this model.

Most often, this kind of intellectual property will be directed to a functional aspect of the technology. When you look at the competitive landscape, you will look for a feature used broadly in the industry and/or in related industries. Since only new technology features are normally suitable for intellectual property coverage, this assessment can be prospective. That is, the intellectual property covers a technology aspect of the product or industry that you expect will become a key aspect in the future.

An Interesting Aspect of These Players: The Break-Out

One of my personal observations on this model for intellectual property is the nature of some of the disputes, that is, the lawsuits. These disputes seem to be particularly contentious with a "winner takes all" mentality. These lawsuits generally are not settled.

This situation is in contrast to other types of industries in which the lawsuit is often a tactic for gaining leverage in an overall negotiation. Settlement is the common outcome in such cases, given the risks to both sides in the dispute.

Importantly, in most intellectual property disputes the accuser's intellectual property also comes up for scrutiny. The result of this scrutiny may be to eliminate the accuser's intellectual property as improperly obtained. Thus, accusers are at risk of losing their own intellectual property.

Note that as described above, if the accuser loses intellectual property rights and copies get to enter the market, all parties can be negatively impacted if they are using a pricing power model. The accused may not want to win that battle.

Among defensive bargainers, however, there seem to be fewer nuances to the disputes. Some may observe that this aggressive approach to litigation parallels the heavy market competition of a fast-paced industry, where "winner takes all while the market is hot" is the whole point.

I think there may be another dynamic. Given the choice, no company would choose a defensive bargaining model over a pricing power model. The nature of the circumstances of the market and fast-paced product development dictate the intellectual property model, not choice.

However, if a leading player in that industry sees an opportunity to break out and achieve a pricing power model (the break-out), they do so aggressively. They are so contentious in their assertion of their rights because that is the whole point. It is no longer a game of mutually assured destruction and has become a game of "winner takes all."

The break-out candidate has been collecting intellectual property in their industry for years, nursing a defensive bargaining position. They have seen the numbers if they can take the whole market, and they want it. Someone has convinced them (probably patent lawyers) that they can have it all without repercussion from their competitors' intellectual property. They go for it.

The outcomes of these kinds of cases can be headline grabbing. The popular awareness of the products and the size of the market drive the drama. A win can be spectacular and a loss can be devastating. There are definitely big winners and losers no matter the outcome of these cases.

A contrast to this approach can be found by the behavior of Motorola in the mobile phone business. In the early days of the mobile telephone industry, methods of pursuing an intellectual property model were still developing. Some of the manufacturers of mobile telephone products viewed intellectual property rights as an unnecessary expense and chose to forgo them.

At the time, manufacturers were mostly familiar with the pricing power model of intellectual property. They accurately saw that this model would not apply to a fast-paced technology industry as effectively as to industries with longer product life-cycles.

Although it is true that mobile telephone products had a very short shelf-life before the next generation was introduced, Motorola chose to build a library of intellectual property around some fundamental concepts used across the generations of the products.

However, Motorola did not pursue a "winner takes all" litigation approach to enforcing these rights. Instead, they chose to pursue another model, described next.

The Third Model: Direct Revenue Generation

The last basic intellectual property model used by a company is direct revenue generation. This approach is to generate revenue by renting or selling intellectual property rights themselves. While any kind of company that generates intellectual property rights can engage the model, it is most commonly suited for technology companies that generate technology but lack the culture to transform that technology into products.

Who Uses the Direct Revenue Generation Model?

Probably the largest industry groups that do this are universities. Scientists, engineers and other creative people working for universities create technology, but often do not have the culture for converting those technologies into products and services. Therefore, many universities have created very sophisticated systems for selling or renting intellectual property rights to these core technologies to generate revenue.

Since they are primarily technology developers, these market players tend to seek intellectual property that describes functional aspects of the technology. They generally find creative, aesthetically related intellectual property unmarketable. They seek customers who are looking to introduce new products or greatly improved products. One exception to this general rule would be contract graphic design artists whose aesthetic products are integrated into the customers' products.

How Does It Work?

Direct revenue generation companies solicit product companies to buy or rent intellectual property related to the products being developed or sold to consumers.

When the intellectual property is directed to new or improved products, buyers can more easily choose to take or refuse the offer. The decision will be purely on their interest in pursuing the new or improved product. The situation gets more complex, however, when the offer includes intellectual property covering a product already being sold by the prospective intellectual property purchaser.

Keep in mind that the prospective purchasers are assessing the value proposition offered by the intellectual property. Prospective buyers can have one of two reactions to the solicitation. If the intellectual property will enhance their exclusivity position, they will be pleased with the offer. If it does not enhance the positioning of their model, they will be less interested.

Intellectual property purchasers' exclusivity positions can be enhanced if the intellectual property offered provides them with the ability to maintain or increase the strength of the intellectual property model they use. This edge may be accomplished by improvements of existing products or by introducing new products with new life-cycles. The new products may be replacements of existing products whose life cycles are expiring or wholly new products.

In particular, companies using the pricing power model can have a particularly positive view of direct revenue generation industries. Remember that pricing power model users are very concerned about the expiration of their rights. When the intellectual property being offered extends exclusivity beyond the buyer's existing intellectual property rights, a pricing power model customer sees a significant value proposition.

However companies that are primarily driven by defensive bargaining models can often see companies using the direct revenue generation model in a completely different light. Keep in mind that defensive bargaining model users are deriving revenue primarily from advanced features in their products. It will not drive their sales and revenues if the intellectual property being offered does not include new technology to advance these features or functionality of a product. Likewise, the intellectual property being offered will have no value to a defensive bargainer if the intellectual property does not meaningfully advance its defensive bargaining position.

Hence, defensive bargaining model users often see direct revenue model users as upstarts and commonly refer to them as trolls. Trolls are perceived as rent seekers siphoning off revenue without adding anything meaningful.

Moreover, the buyer may have difficulty in refusing to purchase the intellectual property they value so little. For example, consider a scenario in which the intellectual property covers a feature of a product that the defensive bargainer is selling. The offer of the intellectual property comes with a veiled threat that nonpayment may lead to a lawsuit against that product.

The target company's defensive bargaining position depends on competitors being vulnerable to being sued in return. However, in this scenario, direct revenue generation companies have no such products. They are not frightened by the intellectual property portfolios of the defensive bargaining companies.

Thus, defensive bargaining industries often do not see value in the acquisition of more intellectual property, yet have no sword or shield against the demands of the direct revenue generation company. The defensive bargaining technique fails against this type of company.

The direct revenue generation company is then labelled a troll. A rent-seeker with nothing of value to offer.

How Do I Identify Intellectual Property as Suitable for the Direct Revenue Generation Model?

Generally, direct revenue generation companies will be leaders in technology development. Their intellectual property will more often than not reflect the next generation of technology.

Intellectual property that fulfills the criteria of the pricing power model for the buyer is the most valuable. That is, the intellectual property that enhances the product life cycle for the company that pays for it.

However, since the features covered are likely directed to the next generation of technology, it may be speculative as to whether or not there is such value today. The more convincing the story as to the value of the new or improved technology and its likelihood of adoption by the market, the more valuable the intellectual property is in this model.

When the intellectual property is relatively old, you will need to assess if it covers existing products. When this is the case, how essential is the feature described to the function of the product and/or the perception of product value to the customer? Does the intellectual property enhance the product seller's ability to maintain or extend an intellectual property advantage through the other two models?

Answers to these questions will provide a reasonable assessment of the suitability of a piece of intellectual property to generate revenue and/or how much revenue is reasonable.

An Interesting Note: The Unicorn

There is a theoretical creature in this model that would be a beautiful sight, but is extremely unlikely to be seen. In this situation, a new technology will generate a product that is so disruptive to the current market that it will change how customers use the products.

In this dream world, the direct revenue generator can offer to a defensive bargaining industry a technology so new and so compelling that all the intellectual property currently held by the competitors in the industry will be obsolete.

This would provide the purchaser with a chance to break-out. The buyer would have a new leading product and all their competitors' intellectual property could not touch them. The buyer may even assert their own current intellectual property against the old products to eliminate any competition.

It would allow a defensive bargainer to convert to a pricing power player.

I relate this possibility not because it is common or even at all likely. Rather, this is the story direct revenue generators always like to tell when they are seeking investment or selling their wares. It rarely plays out as projected, so seek some downside protection in the event such dreams do not come true.

An Interaction of All Three Models

As an exercise, it is helpful to consider the interaction of all three models in a single example. The Motorola example introduced above is suitable.

Though it is true that mobile telephone products have a very short shelf-life before the next generation is introduced, Motorola was able to build a library of intellectual property around some fundamental concepts used across the generations. At first glance, it seems that they were trying to pursue a pricing power model.

However, a pricing power model requires a product producing revenue. It is hard to name a successful Motorola mobile phone product. So, Motorola instead switched to a different model.

Motorola did not try to break-out with their intellectual property. Even though their competitors had little intellectual property at the time to engage as a defensive bargainer, Motorola was missing at least one key component of a break-out. For the same reason they could not apply a pricing power model; even if they asserted their rights aggressively, they had no product with which to capitalize on a win.

Motorola wisely made their money through licensing fees directed to the functional aspects of mobile phones for which they had obtained intellectual property. Their competitors needed Motorola controlled technology to produce the great products.

Mobile phone sellers that had foregone pursuing intellectual property rights (or used a defensive bargaining model) had very little defense when Motorola came knocking on their door telling them they had had to pay for the technology owned by Motorola. Motorola had no product meaningfully at risk in a defensive bargaining environment, so they were bullet-proof in the defensive.

Yet, Motorola was wise enough to understand that a confrontational strategy would not succeed, so they sought reasonable fees for access to their technology on a cooperative basis.

So a potential pricing power model was converted to a direct revenue model and used within a defensive bargaining dominated industry. A key to success was the reasonableness of the demand.

One lesson here is that the product has to keep up with the intellectual property and vice versa to succeed in a pricing power model. Failing that, other models need to be applied to generate revenue.

Now that you better understand how intellectual property can be used in a technology company, you can finally turn to the recognized categories of modern intellectual property…

Chapter 5: Categories of Modern Intellectual Property

So far, you have gained a working understanding of what intellectual property is and how it is used by corporations. It is now time to turn to the recognized categories of intellectual property.

I will not spend much time discussing the individual rules of each category. Those rules are in a constant state of flux, and you are best served by your attorney to keep you informed. However, I will define each category and explore the types of ideas that are allowed to be owned.

There are four primary categories of intellectual property: patents, trademarks, copyrights and trade secrets. I like to add a fifth, less recognized, concept that I refer to as quasi intellectual property. I will explore each category with (1) the types of ideas to which the category gives exclusivity and (2) the ways in which each type is generally used in the context of the three core intellectual property models.

Patents

The first category, patents, is somewhat complex. I will break it down to primary elements. In short, patents cover inventions that come from ideas.

The distinction between an idea and an invention is a very important. Patents cover inventions and only cover ideas to the extent that the ideas are encompassed by the inventions. The difference is described below.

What Are Inventions to be Patented?

As an example, you can imagine that a concave mirror will make your face look larger. However, the mirror can also make your features disproportionate. A mirror that magnifies your face while keeping all of your facial features proportionate would be a great idea.

You may not patent this idea. It is only an idea that cannot be exploited. Disclosure of this idea has no tangible benefit to society at large. In order to receive a patent, you need an invention that achieves the idea you have described. The invention that carries out the idea can be described and patented. The key functional elements that make the mirror work will belong to you for a period of time.

A good example to illustrate this difference is Samuel Morse's telegraph. Morse's goal was to send messages very quickly over long distances. His idea was to achieve this goal by sending electromagnetic signals that could be decoded into letters.

Morse built a device (an invention) that would carry out this function using wire to carry the signals. He received a patent that included not only his specific invention, but also an attempt to achieve exclusivity over the general idea of communication over distance using electromagnetic signals.

The courts decided that his invention was a telegraph, his contribution was a telegraph, and the idea of communicating over a distance using any electromagnetic transmission means was beyond the scope of his invention. He did not invent all methods of communicating using electromagnetic energy. From this example, you can see that to get a patent it is necessary to have working examples of an idea, called inventions.

You can gain exclusivity for your invention if it fulfills a few more criteria, as well. I will leave it to your attorney to fill in the finer details, but at a minimum your invention has to be new and it cannot be obvious. These requirements are meant to ensure that your exclusivity only extends to the new contribution you are making to society.

To make that contribution, you have to put your invention down in writing and drawings. Your description has to include working examples that are functional. You will be granted a period of exclusivity for your use of your invention, but society gains ownership of your invention after the exclusivity expires. Therefore, society needs to be able to know all the critical details of how your invention works.

How Are Patents Used in the Models?

As you recall, the three basic intellectual property models are pricing power, defensive bargaining and direct revenue generation. Patents are useful for all three basic models.

Patents can support the two key criteria of the pricing power model. That is, (1) a patent can cover a key component or functionality of a product, and (2) if that component or functionality is not readily substitutable by consumers, the pricing power model is achieved.

The patent coverage permits increased pricing without a loss of volume or increased volume without a loss of price. The patented technology may support increased volume without a loss of price, if it permits efficiency in production or delivery. The patented technology may support increased price without a loss of sales volume, if it modifies the product itself and increases its value to the consumer.

A patent can support a defensive bargaining model even though it has failed one of the criteria of the pricing power model, as long as the patent describes a feature of a competitor's product. The purpose of using this model is to discourage competitors from seeking to enforce their own patents against the patent holder. If a patent holder is sued, the competitor is at risk of being sued in return by the patent holder under these patents. Competitors are encouraged to fight it out in the marketplace on the merits of the products rather than fighting in the courtroom over the merits of the patents. The courtroom is much more expensive and unpredictable.

Patents can support the direct revenue generation model. The goal is to encourage a product seller to pay you for selling their products which have features covered by your patents.

Often, this conversation takes place in a larger context. As the owner of a patent, you will propose new products or product improvements using technology you have developed. One of the ways of getting paid by the buyers of the new technology is to receive payment for use of the patent rights. Payment terms are connected to the patent and its expiration date, not to the technology directly.

Keep in mind that the value of these patents to buyers depends on how much the patented technology advances their intellectual property model. As a patent holder, you should analyze the buyers' business to assess which intellectual property models the buyers currently use and/or need in the future. How does your intellectual property fit into these models?

For example, buyers are likely to be sensitive to the date on which their own intellectual property will expire if they are using a pricing power model. As a seller or licenser of patents, you should ask yourself whether or not you are offering an extension of that date. Also ask yourself whether or not you are offering patents covering technology to be used in the next generation product. Just as important, does your intellectual property offer the buyer a chance to extend the life cycle of its products or introduce replacements?

There is good value if you are selling an enhancement of the product life cycle to a pricing power user. You are also offering good value, if you are offering defensive bargainers an opportunity to defend themselves against a competitor.

On the other hand, if you are offering patents to defensive bargainers that would only add one more item to a full patent hand, you are offering little value. You run the risk of being labelled a "troll." Reasonableness becomes your watchword.

What if you are targeting a defensive bargainer, but this company is the only one using your patented technology? Your patent will not enhance their defensive bargaining position.

In that case, look at the market for their product. Does your patented feature offer them pricing power value in the market? If not, they are not likely to be your best customer. You are not enhancing their current intellectual property model and not offering a better model.

What if you approach their competitor? Your patent may very well enhance a defensive bargaining model for that customer.

Finally, the most valuable patents for direct revenue generation are the unicorns (Chapter 3). Will the patents permit a defensive bargainer a chance to break-out? Very rare but very valuable.

Trademarks

The second category of intellectual property is trademarks. A trademark is used as a brand for your product.

What Are Trademarks?

Trademarks are generally unique designs or names. The designs can be from a unique mark to a unique design of the packaging. When a manufacturer/seller attaches a unique design and/or name to a product, the consumer can understand who made or sold that product.

It is critical to note that a trademark is not the actual name of a product. For example, Kleenex brand facial tissues use the brand "Kleenex" and the product name "facial tissues." Facial tissues tells you what the product is, and Kleenex tells you who makes and sells the product. A brand does not tell you what a product is; a brand tells you where the product comes from.

Trademark history will help to understand this distinction. Unlike patents, trademarks did not originate as intellectual property rights. Their origin is in laws preventing unfair competition. That is, trademarks were a part of consumer protection law before they became a part of intellectual property rights law.

Keep in mind that when consumers decide how much to spend on a product, the quality of that product is very important to them. Consumers would have very little information from which to differentiate one product from another if all products sat on the shelf in perfectly square, brown cardboard boxes with only their product name.

By affixing a differentiating mark and/or packaging, sellers give consumers an idea of the quality differences among the choices. Over time, consumers will associate some unique marks or packaging with certain levels of quality and features. Their perceptions of quality will create value proposition differences between the products; that is, trademarks can indicate value for products.

Trademarks have now expanded from differentiating marks informing consumers to becoming property rights of the producer or seller. Companies now seek to defend their trademarks and their branding as a property right. Through marketing and advertising, companies raise their brand reputations for quality and identify their brands with the values of their target consumers (cool factor, environmentally sound, and so on).

Because trademarks originated as consumer protection laws, the limitations normally found in intellectual property laws are less well defined. For example, patents have a prescribed and definitive lifetime, but trademark expiration is less clear.

A trademark in the United States can be owned for as long as that trademark is actually used, with periodic reregistrations. Countries outside the United States generally only require fee payment to maintain the rights. But the rights expire if the use or fee ceases.

How Are Trademarks Used in the Models?

Trademarks are well-suited for the pricing power model. They describe an aesthetic feature of a product, fulfilling the first criterion of the model. Trademarks can be the brand, a design or the unique "look and feel" of a product and/or its packaging.

The second criterion of the pricing power model is fulfilled through quality control, marketing and public relations. Companies generate a reputation attractive to target purchasers for quality, coolness, environmental soundness, civic responsibility, and so on. Target customers identify closely with these core values. Therefore, targeted customers are less likely to seek alternatives to this product.

Trademarks are not well suited to the defensive bargaining model. The defensive bargaining model requires intellectual property that covers competitors' products. Because a trademark is unique to your own product, it is very unlikely that a trademark would extend to a competitor's product.

Trademarks are quite well suited to the direct revenue model. Often trademark owners will invest heavily in marketing and public relations to enhance their brands. Brands can even have value outside of a company's core products.

Trademark owners can generate revenue by permitting others to use the marks on their own products to enhance the value of those products to the target market. The popularity of a brand can define the suitability and value of a trademark for licensing out.

Another way to license a trademark is to hire out the brand for the exact same product, but in a market outside of the one in which the brand owner currently sells. For example, it was quite common for Western consumer brands to contract out their trademarks to Chinese companies to sell locally produced products under an international brand name. This approach was cheaper and faster than for the brand owner to learn how to set up and operate directly in China. Often such contracts must come with quality and other restrictions to protect the brand.

Copyrights

The third intellectual property right is copyright. A copyright permits an artist, musician or author to limit others' ability to copy and use works of art. This category of intellectual property rights is one that strays from our general guideline that intellectual property is "the ownership of an idea." In this category, what cannot be copied are the creators' expressions, but not necessarily their underlying ideas.

For example, imagine you were to write a murder mystery. At the end of the novel, you created a very clever notion that the victim's servant was responsible for the murder. In short, the butler did it.

Your book has great success. A large number of followers-on begin writing murder mystery novels in which the butler did it. You are outraged. That was your idea, that was your success, and these other authors are riding your coattails. Does copyright provide you with an intellectual property right by which you can declare exclusivity to that idea in your novel?

The answer is no. Copyright laws protect you against the direct copying of the *expression* of your ideas. The descriptive language that you used and the characters that you created, along with the ways in which the characters interacted, are protected. The underlying *idea* that the victim was murdered by the butler has no such protection. There must be direct copying or copying of a number of creative elements of your novel to have violated your rights.

Like patents, copyrights are a defined-term intellectual property right that from initiation have clear expiration dates. However, there is a wrinkle in that some copyrighted works have an extremely high value to both the company that owns them and to society at large.

The core Disney characters are a prime example of this situation. Their value is very high and the loss of exclusivity would be very significant to both the company and to the economy at large. When copyright on the Disney characters come close to expiration, the legislature tends to extend all copyright expirations. The latest such law was passed in 1998 and was derisively referred to as the "Mickey Mouse Act." It is unclear when this series of extensions may end.

How Are Copyrights Used in the Models?

Copyrights are nearly identical to trademarks in their use in the models. They are well-suited for use in the pricing power model. They cover specific expressions of words and art, so the first criterion is fulfilled.

As for substitutability (the second criterion), that is within the core nature of art itself. The more compelling the expression to the audience, the less desirable substitutions are to the patrons of art.

Copyrights are less suited for a defensive bargaining model. Copyright coverage is specific to an expression. Direct copies or obvious derivatives are covered. It is unlikely that a copyright will have coverage so broad as to encompass a competitor who does not copy or create derivatives.

The direct revenue model provides opportunity for copyright holders. This model is the basis for book royalties, theater tickets, and so on. Your theater or concert ticket is a license (sale of limited rights) to view an expression of the entertainment. Copyrights offer the mechanism to control the copying of books, art or performances. Copyrights provide the ownership rights in the art that permit the copyright holder to conduct trade and make money from that art.

Trade Secrets

The next area of intellectual property rights is trade secrets. Trade secrets rights were not granted by Congress under the Constitution and do not have set expiration dates. The rights to the secrets expire when the secrets become publicly known. Theoretically these intellectual property rights could last forever. Just as possibly, however, they might last only five minutes.

The most famous trade secret is the recipe for Coca-Cola, a secret that has outlasted all others. However, should that secret ever become legally known, that property right would be forever lost.

How Do Trade Secrets Work?

A company will keep a key piece of information secret as long as it can. Sales brochures and other publications will never reveal the secret. Employees and business partners will sign agreements to keep the secret.

A competitor to a trade secret owner may use any legal means available to learn the secret. However, if a competitor engages in illegal acts, the courts will support the trade secret owner in seeking compensation for lost property.

Nevertheless, trade secrets are fair game. Competitors actively seek to learn those secrets when they can. Most often, competitors will review publicly available information to glean the secret, engage in reverse engineering of a product, or just stumble upon the same notion that underlies the secret. When competitors succeed legally, the trade secret is over.

Who Uses Trade Secrets?

Companies interested in trade secrets tend to use them to bypass the expiration dates of standard intellectual property rights. This approach flies in the face of the concept that we want to encourage innovators to disclose their ideas so that society as a whole may benefit. However, that is a voluntary system and a relatively narrow band of innovations are suitable for trade secret protection.

After all, many competitors reverse engineer everything associated with a product to learn its secrets. Some secrets might involve an aspect of the product that is subject to reverse engineering or public disclosure through government regulation. Hence, such aspects of the product are not good candidates for trade secret protection.

Trade secrets are particularly valuable for inventions that do not receive adequate protection under the patent system. For example, many manufacturing methods for creating products can be quite valuable. Imagine that you invented a method for greatly decreasing the amount of time it takes give whiskey a genuine aged flavor. It would be difficult to know if your competitors were using the same method. This is especially true if you are competing internationally. You cannot enforce a patent right against your competitor if you do not know what that competitor is doing behind closed doors.

Moreover, the patent system requires you to write down and publish your invention in return for your exclusivity rights. Your competitors will know all about your method even before your exclusivity rights begin. There will be little or no way to know whether or not your competitors are using your method. Using patents, it would be very difficult to enforce your exclusivity rights against them.

Under these circumstances, most companies will forgo seeking patents for such inventions and choose to keep them secret. Companies set up systems to protect them as trade secrets.

How Are Trade Secrets Used in the Models?

Trade secrets are well-suited to the pricing power model. Methods of manufacture and other aspects that are not easily reverse engineered are particularly suitable. Their value is self-evident, otherwise there would be no need to keep them secret. Most likely the technology being kept secret reduces the investment and/or time to get a product to market. Increased efficiency allows for higher profit.

However, fulfilling both criteria of the pricing power model are necessary if the trade secret covers something intrinsic to the final product. For example, the recipe for Coca Cola is not easily reverse engineered, but it has a direct impact on the flavor of the final product. Therefore, criterion two, assessing the ease of substitution of alternatives (e.g., other flavors), becomes essential to the effectiveness in a pricing power model.

As for the defensive bargaining model, trade secrets are nearly non-existent. It is next to impossible to seek to extend trade secret protection beyond direct copies of your specific products/methods. This is particularly true when enforcement of the trade secret would require disclosure of that same secret.

Trade secrets are often used in direct revenue models. Monetizing a trade secret using contracts that also protect the secret are easily accomplished. Trade secrets can sometimes be applied across product lines or even across industries. Commercialization of the trade secret to its full potential will likely require multiple partnerships.

Quasi Intellectual Property

The last category is not widely recognized as intellectual property rights. It can be referred to as quasi intellectual property rights. Intellectual property concepts can be applied to identify ways in which to create exclusivity zones without using the four main categories of intellectual property.

The most common source of quasi intellectual property is through government action. For example, if you are a car manufacturer and the government introduces complex and very expensive technological requirements for the manufacture of cars, you have now experienced a raising of the barrier for new competition. You can now assess the impact of these regulations for their value in one of the three intellectual property models.

Another government action that can confer quasi intellectual property rights is the requirement to use your product. Presently, the United States government requires that a percentage of the fuel sold for the use of automobiles be ethanol. Companies producing ethanol, and the farmers growing the grain used to make the ethanol, are given a relatively secure market.

These government-created quasi intellectual property rights, however, tend to be supportive to an industry as a whole as opposed to an individual company. Nevertheless, there is value in exclusivity spread to an entire industry, at least against competing products offered by other industries.

Individual companies can also seek to create quasi intellectual property rights to create a zone of exclusivity around their individual products. Most often this is done through contracting with sources for raw materials to obtain the best prices or exclusive sourcing. Likewise, a company may seek exclusive sales contracts with all or most of the customers in a market.

On the other side of this coin is government reaction to such exclusivity agreements. Antitrust laws were designed specifically to counter these kinds of actions. Companies still take these types of actions, but must be very careful when they do so.

Keep in mind that the idea of exclusivity for a company is based upon a balance of the interests of the company and the interests of society at large. Some quasi intellectual property actions taken by the company do not provide a benefit to society. These actions are more likely to be illegal. This is especially true with exclusive customer and exclusive supply agreements that control too much of the market.

So far you have gained a working understanding of what intellectual property is, why it exists, the models corporations use to implement intellectual property, and the different categories of intellectual property. You can now explore an exercise that captures all of these concepts in a spreadsheet or database. With this tool, you can evaluate your strategic intellectual property goals and assess your current positioning relative to those goals. The information you will gain from this exercise will provide a basis for a dashboard display of the intellectual property goals and status.

The intellectual property plan provides a starting point for converting your intellectual property management from a pull system to a push system. Senior management will no longer only pull operational information from the lawyers and ask for guidance. Senior management can now push strategic direction to the lawyers and evaluate intellectual property operational effectiveness against their strategic goals.

Chapter 6: The Intellectual Property Plan

In the previous chapters you learned what intellectual property is, why it exists, how it is used, and the general categories of intellectual property. With this information, you can develop an intellectual property plan.

An intellectual property plan is a living document embodying all the critical parameters for understanding, developing, and managing the intellectual property of a company. There are three phases for creating and using an intellectual property plan. The first phase is a background assessment. The second phase is an analysis phase. The last phase is an implementation phase.

Importantly, this process requires multidisciplinary input. You will need input and guidance from different functions in the company for all three phases. At a minimum, participation will be necessary from senior management as well as legal, marketing, and product development departments.

Each organization will have its own best practices for developing and using an intellectual property plan. Nevertheless, I can describe a general method for developing an intellectual property plan.

Phase 1: Prepare the Background Section

In phase 1, you produce a background statement. This background provides the perspective necessary to understand which intellectual property rights are desirable. You also start to develop the context in which to understand how each piece of intellectual property will apply to the company's strategic needs.

Section 1: The Intellectual Property Models

You start by analyzing each current product (or prospective product) of the business separately.

You will need to identify all the desired intellectual property models by product. One way to accomplish this is to benchmark the models used by other market players in the industry and in related industries.

However, do not miss opportunities to disrupt the norm. A study of your intended positioning of your product in the market may show a desire for using intellectual property models that are not the norm for your industry. If your market positioning disrupts the norm, then your intellectual property usage may also need to disrupt the norm.

Next you should list by product all of the intellectual property models that you have identified as desirable. Be sure to briefly note how that model is implemented. They should be listed in order of importance.

For example, imagine you were competing in the mobile phone market and Apple was your guide. As this industry has primarily defensive bargaining players, you would seek intellectual property to technology that has applicability to your competitors' products.

You would also want to use a pricing power model as your secondary model. You will need unique design (i.e., trademark) to attach to your products. Your investment in the reputation of that mark would include high product quality and ease of use. Eventually, you would seek to have that reputation become so strong that the purchase of your product becomes a status symbol to your customers.

When your company intends to apply more than one intellectual property model to a product or product line, rank the models in order of importance.

In this instance, you would list your models as: (1) defensive bargaining model with intellectual property directed to functional features of the competitors' products and (2) pricing power model suing intellectual property directed to unique aesthetic features of the product (e.g., the trademark). You would also note a need for heavy investment in quality and consistency across products and product models to support the pricing power model.

Section 2: Current State of the Market

Next, describe the solution your product or service is directed toward and the general expected size of the market. Immediately following that, describe your current market share and expected market share. As a guide, create a pie chart showing comparative market shares that include at least your three nearest competitors.

At the end of phase 1, you will have assessed your desired intellectual property model and what you want to achieve in the market. Compare these two goals and assess whether or not there are inconsistencies.

For example, are you expecting to be a strongly dominant player in the market? If so, do you expect to achieve that with a direct revenue model? Since the direct revenue model implies that you are not directly selling a product and are only receiving a portion of revenues of another company, it is likely that these two goals are inconsistent.

Phase 2: The Dashboard Display

In this section, you will create a summary of your company's current intellectual property. This document will be in the form of a chart. Ideally, the chart should be in the form of entries in a database, but a spreadsheet or even word processor table will suffice.

To help you understand how to complete the chart, I will describe creating a chart for a fictional product. The fictional product is a window cleaner with the brand name "Windiz." There are two unique aspects of the product. These are its brand name and a special trigger spray mechanism with an "arrester" that prevents overspray of the product outside of a narrow band. Customers really like that they can spray the cleaner without worrying about overspray damaging nearby wood, fabrics or other delicate materials.

The product has one piece of intellectual property for each of these unique features. The first feature (its unique brand name) has a trademark registration. The second feature (the trigger mechanism) has a patent registration. There is one row in the chart for each piece of intellectual property.

The first column of the chart is the "product name" column. The next column is the "intellectual property type" column (e.g., patent, trademark, copyright, or trade secret).

In the Windiz example, the first row will list "Windiz," in the product name column and "trademark" in the intellectual property type column. From now on I will refer to this as the trademark row.

In the second row, "Windiz" will be listed in the product name column and "patent" will be listed in the intellectual property type column. From now on I will refer to this as the patent row.

Product	IP Type
Windiz	Trademark
Windiz	Patent

The next column is the "intellectual property description" column. This is a short description of the technical scope of the intellectual property.

In this column you describe the intellectual property coverage that is relevant to the product's feature(s). Examples might include the brand name, a brief description of the functional component of the product, aesthetic features and so on. Your intellectual property attorney should assist in this step.

In our Windiz example, the trademark row of the table will have "Windiz" in the intellectual property description column. This indicates that the trademark as registered with the government is the unique word "Windiz."

In the patent row, the language should summarize the patent coverage as: "nozzle with overspray arrestor." As you can see, a summary of the patent coverage relevant to the product is listed here. Again, your attorney can assist on this step.

Product	IP Type	IP Description
Windiz	Trademark	"Windiz"
Windiz	Patent	Nozzle with overspray arrestor

The next column is the "coverage" column and indicates whether or not the intellectual property covers the product you sell. Typically this is a yes/no answer, and your intellectual property attorney can assist you.

In our example, in the trademark row the coverage column should list a "Y". In the patent row would also show a "Y". I have now designated that both pieces of intellectual property cover the product.

Product	IP Type	IP Description	Cover?
Windiz	Trademark	"Windiz"	Y
Windiz	Patent	Nozzle with overspray arrestor	Y

The next column is the "intellectual property model" column and lists the intellectual property models suited to this piece of intellectual property.

If the coverage column lists a "Y", then consider the pricing power model and/or the defensive bargaining model. The direct revenue model may also be suitable.

If the coverage column lists an "N", then only the defensive bargaining model and/or direct revenue models are suitable. Defensive bargaining is suitable if the intellectual property covers a competitor's product and you intend to hold this intellectual property defensively to discourage patent litigation from that competitor. The direct revenue model is suitable if the intellectual property covers another company's product or offers a product improvement, and you intend to seek payment from that company for using your technology.

In my example, for the trademark row I could choose the pricing power model if the company intends to invest in the reputation of the brand. The investment would be in quality control and/or marketing. A strong reputation for quality, coolness, environmental soundness, civic responsibility and so on can add to the value proposition in the mind of the buyer.

On the other hand, I might also choose the direct revenue model as an alternate or in addition to the pricing power model. It is an alternate choice if the company does not intend to be the only manufacturer/seller using the brand. In that case, the trademark could be offered to others to place on their products.

For the patent row in my example chart, I will very likely list the pricing power model in the intellectual property column. The patent covers my product and allows me to prevent others from using my arrester on their products.

I might, however, choose the defensive bargaining model if my competitors are using this feature, but they have intellectual property that covers other features of my product. I could hold this intellectual property to discourage those competitors from suing me under their patents.

I could also list the direct revenue model. This approach is particularly appropriate, for example, if this arrester is useful on products outside of window cleaner. Even though I am not making those products, perhaps the makers of these other products would be willing to pay a fee to use my arrester technology (e.g., prevent overspray of weed killer).

Product	IP Type	IP Description	Cover?	Model
Windiz	Trademark	"Windiz"	Y	PP, DR
Windiz	Patent	Nozzle with overspray arrestor	Y	PP, DR

The next column is the "status" column where you note whether or not this piece of intellectual property is pending approval by the government or is currently registered and in effect. Registration status is particularly relevant to patents and trademarks where government review and approval is necessary. It takes time to get through the process (sometimes years).

Product	IP Type	IP Description	Cover?	Model	Status
Windiz	Trademark	"Windiz"	Y	PP, DR	Issued
Windiz	Patent	Nozzle with overspray arrestor	Y	PP, DR	Pend.

Uncertainty in the outcome of this process could cause uncertainty in the suitable intellectual property model. After all, if the patent key to the pricing power model fails to get issued by the government, then the model will also fail.

Finally, the last column is the "expiration date" column in which you note when this piece of intellectual property expires.

Product	IP Type	IP Description	Cover?	Model	Status	Exp.
Windiz	Trademark	"Windiz"	Y	PP, DR	Issued	10/2020 Renewable
Windiz	Patent	Nozzle with overspray arrestor	Y	PP, DR	Pend.	9/2035

You may choose to add columns as necessary to capture more information, such as unique identifiers (e.g., application numbers). Be as creative as you like, but also try to keep the chart simple. You are creating a dashboard display of complex information, so it is best to keep the dashboard as clear and concise as possible.

A row of the chart should be filled out for each piece of intellectual property in the company's possession. Even intellectual property that has no product to cover and/or no intellectual property model suitable for it needs to be listed.

When you finish the chart, review it for common errors. The most common error is failing to list some of your intellectual property at all. That is, when you are done you find that the company owns intellectual property that did not get onto the chart. This will not be surprising, and likely comes from one of three sources.

The first source is if you made a mistake in the chart. You may have intellectual property covering your competitors' products that is suitable for a defensive bargaining model. You may have missed listing this intellectual property because you were focused on listing intellectual property that would have a "Y" in the coverage column. That is, you were listing intellectual property serving a desired pricing power model and missed intellectual property that is suited for a defensive bargaining model.

As you can see, this mistake can happen when the intellectual property you failed to list does not serve the intellectual property model you desire. However, you need to list all intellectual property related to the product.

The second source is if you have intellectual property that is not associated at all with your or a competitor's products. Yet, the intellectual property may be interesting to other companies (e.g., non-competitors). Perhaps this intellectual property is useful in a direct revenue model. Companies pursuing a pricing power model often overlook this type of intellectual property and miss revenue opportunities.

If you have intellectual property useful for a direct revenue model, list these pieces of intellectual property in the chart. However, in the product name column, list the target companies' names instead of a product name. You can note direct revenue generation in the intellectual property models column.

The third source is that the company has been wasting its money. This is very common when intellectual property is being pursued but it has no bearing on the business in any way; it serves no intellectual property model. Often this happens when the registration process for intellectual property gets disconnected from product development.

Moreover, employee turnover can result in changes in products and product positioning that are not captured in the intellectual property efforts. Give serious consideration to whether or not staff time and money should continue to be spent on this intellectual property. Perhaps the intellectual property efforts need to be redirected.

MILESTONE 1: PERSPECTIVE ON YOUR INTELLECTUAL PROPERTY EFFORTS

At this point, you have reached a milestone in intellectual property management. The chart you created has given you a perspective on which model you should pursue and whether or not you are adequately pursuing that model.

Refer back to the results of Phase 1. Compare the intellectual property model goal for the product to those models you have listed in Phase 2. Do any of the intellectual property models listed match the goal? Is there any intellectual property listed that is outside the intended model?

If you find intellectual property that is outside the intended model, consider whether or not your current intellectual property is supporting the wrong model. Were you wrong about the models available for this product? Should you change the manner in which you invest in your product or in your intellectual property?

Answer these questions carefully and with the support of your intellectual property attorney. Sometimes as little as a single piece of intellectual property can support a strong pricing power model. On the other hand, a hundred pieces of intellectual property may not support any model for your product.

After this assessment you can create your dashboard view. Include in your dashboard a summary of which intellectual property rights support your goals. You should note whether or not this intellectual property is fully registered or pending registration. You can also offer suggestions on future actions to solidify your intellectual property position through intellectual property registrations and/or product marketing or positioning.

MILESTONE 2: PERSPECTIVE ON YOUR PRODUCT LIFE CYCLE

You can now assess whether or not your intellectual property has a serious impact on your product life cycle.

How long will your product be on the market and able to command the current revenue? How long before competition from copiers will reduce your revenue? Sometimes this answer is driven by the intellectual property instead of technical improvements or changing customer interests.

For example, if you are pursuing a pricing power model, then the expiration of the intellectual property supporting that model could define the life cycle of your product. If you are using the direct revenue generation model, then the expiration of the intellectual property is the expiration of your product life-cycle.

How will you avoid the loss of market share and revenue through the loss of this intellectual property? If your products become legally copied by competitors due to these expirations, valuable improvements in the product or replacement products having improved features may be necessary.

When you are using a pricing power model, you may also need to have a look at your competitors' intellectual property. When you are competing with only a few players and each of the competing products are fairly substitutable, the first one losing its intellectual property will affect all other players (see Chapter 4). The life cycle of your product may be defined by your competitors' intellectual property expiration dates if they predate your own.

You should look carefully at preparations to introduce a new product. Alternatively, you can invest in teaching the market that your product is not as similar to your competitors' as it may appear.

The truth is, when you are using a pricing power model, life cycle management is the life of your company, and the exercise in this chapter can be an essential component of managing your company's revenue.

Regardless of which model(s) you are using, make a note in your dashboard as to the expected life-cycle of your current product(s) and what drives that date. You should decide how that life-cycle should be managed.

Phase 3: The Plan for the Future

At this point, your plan for future action is already in your dashboard. You have reviewed your current status and listed what actions are necessary to support and/or improve your intellectual property model(s). You have also listed the current status and what actions may be necessary to manage your product life-cycle(s).

The complexity of the plan is variable. It can be a simple marketing support of the present value proposition. Alternatively, it may be a call to action to completely change the intellectual property model pursued for the product. Either way, you have captured all the key elements in the dashboard. Specific operational actions flow from there.

THE END:

This book has taught you how to understand what intellectual property is, why it exists, how it is used, what categories exist and how to create a dashboard display of your intellectual property efforts. You should now be able to ascertain (1) whether or not you are pursuing the right intellectual property model, (2) whether or not you are pursuing the intellectual property model that you intend, and (3) how your intellectual property affects your product life cycle. I hope that you find this information, and this book, very useful.

Afterword

I want to thank you for reading this book. I hope that you found it a useful description of intellectual property management.

I want you to have the background knowledge and the tools to begin to treat your intellectual property as assets and manage them well. You should be able to direct your advisors and lawyers more actively instead of waiting for them to report their understandings of your intellectual property situation.

There is so much more to intellectual property management, but this book should get you started.

If this book was helpful to you, please let me know and let others know, as well. Feel free to pose any questions that come up when you read this book. If there is interest, perhaps I will produce a second book with insights on more complex and comprehensive intellectual property management techniques.

Good luck!

Made in the USA
Monee, IL
04 November 2026

67385825R00046